PiVOTAL
BEHAViOUR
MANAGEMENT
HANDBOOK

© Text copyright Paul Dix 2005
© Photographs copyright Pivotal Education Ltd 2005

ISBN 0-9549926-0-1

Published by **Pivotal Education Ltd**
6 French Gardens, Lindfield, West Sussex, RH16 2EF

CONTENTS

FOREWORD

(Please note that for the duration of the handbook I have chosen to write all teachers as feminine and all pupils as masculine, to save on confusion)

When you see a good teacher in the classroom, her behaviour management seems effortless. Her classes are often relaxed and good humoured, the students are attentive and engaged in the learning, relationships are positive and there is mutual trust in the room. Students who are challenging elsewhere in the school seem to have undergone a miraculous transformation. Other staff accept that the teacher has orderly classes but often attribute this to the strength of her personality, her time in the school or her physical presence in the room. Her behaviour management skills are rarely discussed because they are applied so discreetly that they are difficult to identify, let alone emulate.

Yet teachers like this have not woken up one day with the gift of good behaviour management. What are the skills that they have honed over time? What strategies are disguised by the fluency of their teaching? How do they get through an entire lesson without breaking out in a rash brought on by stress?

I spent long hours preparing schemes of work and lesson plans in anticipation of starting my first post. I thought hard about the students I would be teaching and how to engage them in an exciting educational adventure with me at the helm. Lever-arch files in hand stuffed with carefully prepared resources, I skipped to my first class ready to educate and inspire. I was confident, well prepared and eager to impress. The students, however, had their own agenda. They had been taught by supply teachers for the last two terms and had very different expectations of their new teacher. Within five minutes of starting the class, two had climbed out of the window, one was swinging on the curtains and the others could not be persuaded to interrupt their game of table football, which was by now reaching fever pitch. I called for help and the Head of Year arrived.

Silence and calm descended in an instant. The students listened intently to him, and with coats off and pens out, we were now ready to start the lesson. As he left I thanked him and turned to address the class who, sensing his departure, had returned to their former pursuits; a penalty shoot waits for no man. Driving home after that first day I was close to tears. I resolved to seek out those teachers who had the skills that I was lacking and learn them...quickly.

It was to those early mentors that I owe so much. Their classes were lovely places to be, positive, caring and full of good humour and focused learning. They showed me how to:

» **communicate my expectations to the students explicitly**
» **gain a perspective on my emotional state**
» **empathise with students' individual needs**
» **remain consistent and fair**
» **manage confrontation and challenging conversations**
» **use praise and positive reinforcement instead of constant sanctions**
» **build relationships with students who present the full range of challenging behaviours**

Through them I learned that accepting support was not a sign of weakness but a necessary stage in my learning. It also served to demonstrate to the students that I was not alone but part of a strong team working to help them make better choices.

I wondered how long it would take for me to gain the respect that those mentors had. Two months after my arrival, the Headteacher was relieved of his post and within a year the school was placed into Special Measures. It wasn't until the end of the first year that I began teaching some truly effective lessons. After four years of learning and additional training, I was leading the whole staff in implementing a new behaviour management policy and my entrance into a classroom now had a similar effect as had the Year Head's on that first day. I had cracked it. It was time to move on to a new post at a three site inner city school in Birmingham. I approached this new post brimming with confidence; after all I had behaviour management down to a fine art and had been there and bought the T-shirt years before.

Walking into my first class, full of the skills of an experienced teacher, I could not understand why the students were not listening, why silence had not descended and why the same panic my first ever lesson had elicited was rising inside me. A difficult day turned into a difficult week and a difficult first term. I could not see what had gone wrong. Slowly I realised that these students did not know my rules, my expectations and, most frustratingly, they didn't know that their teacher was one of the good ones. After sifting through my notes and reflections I returned to the strategies that had helped me in the past. Gradually I began to translate the skills I had learnt in the previous school to my new post. A valuable lesson was learnt: even as a Head of Faculty it was vital to concentrate on the basics, the strategies that I knew worked. It is these key training points that the Pivotal Behaviour Management Handbook is designed to share.

This handbook has been designed to enable you gradually to improve the management of behaviour in your classroom. It outlines the vital skills and strategies that effective teachers are using in their classrooms every day. As a teacher you need time to implement and integrate these skills. You should focus on a new section each week and then look at integrating the skills into your own teaching style. The course is designed to allow you to learn actively with tasks to complete after each training section. Each section explains the principles behind the practice, how it works in the classroom, what to watch out for in the early stages and the first steps for implementation in your own classroom.

HOW TO USE THIS HANDBOOK

This handbook is designed for individual teachers to use and does not rely on or prescribe a whole school approach. Read the book through to the end. Spend some time thinking about the issues that it raises for your own practice. Then re-read and complete the training activity on one section every week while trying the strategies with students. Allow yourself time to think through, practise and implement the strategies. You may want to focus on one class as a 'pilot' group before introducing the techniques to all of your classes; perhaps start with the class that you currently have least difficulty with.

Don't expect your new skills to work first time or every time. This course is a fast-track introduction to techniques that you will hone over time and throughout your career. With professionalism and diligence the approaches explained in this handbook will work. They are being used right now in schools all over the UK even with the most challenging students.

Keep using the strategies; be dogged and relentless in your pursuit of calmer, better managed and more enjoyable classes.

As your first step answer the true/false questions and add comments to explain your response. It will help clarify your current views on Behaviour Management and allow you to re-examine your current philosophy. My thoughts and responses to these questions can be found on **www.pivotaleducation.com**

TRUE OR FALSE?

Parents should teach their children how to behave.　T ☐ F ☐
_____
_____

Boys are generally more disruptive than girls.　T ☐ F ☐
_____
_____

The behaviour of my classes is a
reflection of me as a teacher.　T ☐ F ☐
_____
_____

Students from different cultures learn differently.　T ☐ F ☐
_____
_____

How I feel affects the way I teach.　T ☐ F ☐
_____
_____

Children do not need to be thanked
for behaving well in class.　T ☐ F ☐
_____
_____

Good teachers never have problems with students.　T ☐ F ☐
_____
_____

Human beings are motivated by reward.   T ☐ F ☐

_____

_____

Consistency is the key to managing behaviour.   T ☐ F ☐

_____

_____

It is acceptable to shout at children
to get them to behave.   T ☐ F ☐

_____

_____

Children who don't attend regularly deserve to fail.   T ☐ F ☐

_____

_____

People learn best when they are
in a trusting relationship.   T ☐ F ☐

_____

_____

Fear is a useful control mechanism in the classroom.   T ☐ F ☐

_____

_____

The management of behaviour is different
from the management of learning.   T ☐ F ☐

_____

_____

CHAPTER 1:
THiNGS TO THiNK ABOUT
BEFORE YOU START

LESSON PLANNiNG

I am addressing "Lesson Planning" first because it is, without a doubt, the most important point.

The quality of your planning will have a direct effect on the behaviour in your classroom and whilst this handbook can address the management of behaviour it does not seek to do so in isolation. Give yourself a fair chance to manage behaviour in your classes by planning carefully to ensure successful learning is taking place. Poor planning of learning activities will make behaviour management an uphill struggle from the start of the lesson. Do away with worksheets, cloze procedures (fill in the gaps), word-searches, copying from the book or board, schemes that you have no ownership of and any other planning and preparation shortcuts. Your students will know that they are being 'occupied' and respond accordingly. Instead be creative in your planning. Plan lessons that engage the students in their learning. Take some risks, small ones at first and try a more active approach. Get them on their feet and doing as well as in their seats and working. Active learning works. Howard Gardner's work on Multiple Intelligences is essential reading for anyone who wants to understand why and how (read it in his own words first as some of the work that uses the same terminology reinterprets and even misrepresents his research and findings). Also students really appreciate the change to their routine that an active task gives. Just follow a Year 9 student round for the day, and you will be surprised, and shocked, at just how many lessons follow the 'sit down and work, I'll be at my desk' approach.

If your planning and preparation of lessons is not immediately appreciated or students respond negatively to lessons that you have spend a great deal of time on, tempting you to say 'I spent hours on those discussion cards and you kick them round the room/rip them/eat them!' don't give up. It takes time to change the expectations and learning habits that students have built up about what should happen in a lesson. As with behaviour management you have to play the 'long game' and not expect immediate or even short term gains.

Examine your schemes of work, lesson plans and resources carefully.

» **Do they match your students' ability and interests?**
» **Are they relevant, stimulating, dynamic and differentiated?**
» **Do they challenge pupils to think in different ways?**
» **Are lessons planned with timings recorded and pace in mind?**
» **Have you taken into account different learning styles and cultures?**
» **Do your lessons provide opportunities for individual, paired and group work?**
» **Is there space for autonomous and active learning?**
» **Do you build in opportunities for self, peer and group assessment?**

Prepare lessons that do not rely on you holding the attention of the whole class for more than 10 minutes of a 50 minute lesson. Strictly limit the time you spend talking to the whole class. Time yourself; you may be shocked at just how long you are expecting them to listen actively. In all of my observations, extended 'teacher talk time' is a major cause of disruptive behaviour and restless students. Try to set up activities that enable you to practise your behaviour management strategies with individuals and small groups. Consider preparing instructions for learning activities in written form for the students, so that lessons rely less and less on you addressing the whole class.

SCHOOL POLICY AND PRACTICE

>> Check your school's Behaviour Policy. Some of the decisions on school wide classroom rules, sanctions and rewards may have been made for you and you will be able to dovetail your learning rituals with these.

>> Familiarise yourself with the procedure for calling for support from a senior colleague during lesson time. If there is no school policy, make a laminated card that explains that you need immediate assistance. When this need arises, you can send the card to the school office with a reliable student. You might need to make an arrangement with your head of department/area, head of year/key stage or other appropriate colleague.

YOUR CLASSROOM

>> Arrange your classroom so that you can get to each student quickly and easily without disturbing or moving others.

>> Designate areas of the classroom for Behaviour Management displays. Make sure that they are not obscured from view by your desk or cupboards. You may wish to prepare these in advance; it will gently introduce students to the changes that you are going to make and make it easy for you to put new rules, rituals and notices up quickly.

YOUR CLASSES

>> Have a seating plan for all new classes and keep it under constant review. You can use this as part of your negotiation in rewards and sanctions.

If you haven't yet learned the students' first names give them a label to wear until you have (younger students can make badges). Learn the names as soon as possible; the students will remember yours immediately and addressing students as 'You' or 'Red Jumper' is not a good start to a productive relationship.

A QUICK SELF AUDIT OF YOUR CURRENT PRACTICE:

	ALWAYS	SOMETIMES	RARELY	NEVER
I shout at students	☐	☐	☐	☐
I worry that I may have been too harsh on a student	☐	☐	☐	☐
I am consistent in managing behaviour	☐	☐	☐	☐
I tell students the rules for my classroom	☐	☐	☐	☐
I plan what I am going to say to students in conversations about behaviour	☐	☐	☐	☐
The hard working students get forgotten	☐	☐	☐	☐
I find myself in unpleasant confrontations with students	☐	☐	☐	☐
I focus on rewarding good behaviour	☐	☐	☐	☐
I chase up students who miss deadlines and detentions	☐	☐	☐	☐
I communicate with parents about behaviour issues	☐	☐	☐	☐
I seek support and advice on dealing with students with challenging behaviour	☐	☐	☐	☐

CHAPTER 2:
MANAGING YOUR OWN BEHAVIOUR:
THE EMOTIONALLY SECURE CLASSROOM

THE PRINCIPLE

In order to manage the emotional behaviour of your students you need to provide them with a strong model of appropriate emotional responses. This should be your primary focus as a 'role model'. You need to demonstrate and be explicit about how you, as an example of a successful learner deal with your own emotional responses and keep them in check. Students need to feel emotionally secure in your classroom to use the rational part of their brain to address learning challenges. A learning environment that relies on emotional responses from the teacher to manage behaviour is a difficult and often frightening place in which to learn.

THE PRACTICE

Monitor and check your own behaviour in front of the class. This is particularly important when getting to know a new group of students. They are watching for your reactions and may be testing when emotion takes the place of reason in your reactions; they want to know how to 'push your buttons'. Make a resolution not to shout or show anger as a part of your teaching style. There will be times when you need to raise your voice or shout to prevent a dangerous situation but these should only be exceptions to the rule. When you shout at students (and all humans) they feel threatened and their reflex reaction will be 'fight or flight'. The emotional brain takes over and the rational part of their brain that they need for higher order thought is temporarily blocked. That is why shouting 'ANSWER THE QUESTION' rarely gets a positive response.

Model the behaviour that you want to see in your students. Arrive on time for your lessons, prepared for and enthusiastic about learning. Try not to show negative emotional reactions to the class when you are confronting undesirable behaviour but instead explain your frustration as calmly and clearly as possible. You do not need to do this immediately. 'When I walked away from our discussion about the mess on your table I did so because you made me cross. I gave myself time think and work out what to say to you. We now need to have a polite conversation and find a solution to the problem'. Leave your purely emotional reactions for the privacy of home or friends where you are not the role model.

Your students are trying to learn how to deal with their feelings; they need you to model explicitly how you deal with your own. Remember that students may have learned emotional reactions and outbursts from home that are not appropriate in your classroom. I had a student who would persistently shout at me and other students during lessons for no apparent reason. It wasn't until I visited his home to talk to his parents about it that I realised it was not an angry response. There was no volume control in his family at all. They all spoke very loudly, all of the time, regardless of the proximity of others. It took a long while for him to find an appropriate 'voice for the classroom' and understand my expectations. Don't challenge students' prior learning openly but do so by providing a strong model for appropriate behaviour.

Think carefully about how you create a learning environment where all students feel emotionally secure and have the time, opportunity and space to think and speak freely. Examine your most basic routines. When you finish giving instructions for a task add: 'Is there anyone who has any questions about this task? Please ask now, if you don't understand as it may be because I haven't explained it properly and that is my fault'. It will encourage students who are still unsure about the task to ask questions without feeling they are at fault. When students have difficulty answering a question in front of the class try, 'Take a moment to calm down and work out what answer you are going to give. I don't mind if it doesn't come out right first time. You know I don't always say things clearly the first time.' Try to make them feel safe enough to take a risk with their answer.

Give students 'thinking time' to prepare their answers before any hands go up. Try reducing the use of 'hands up', which relies on a few quick thinkers and makes everyone else feel either inadequate or slow. (Are 'fast thinkers' really better than 'slow thinkers'? Surely it's the answer that is important). Consider introducing more subtle rituals for attracting the attention of the teacher. I often use, 'Look at me when you have the answer, look away while you are thinking'. Students enjoy the discreet nature of the communication and everyone gets the space to think.

You might prefer to start exploring some of these ideas by focusing on a small group of students rather than the whole class. As well as introducing some of the new language and frameworks, share with these students some of the ways in which you control your emotional responses when you are learning. Let them see you count to 10, take deep breaths, pace the room or whatever method you use to keep your emotions in check. Talk to them about their learning, how they feel when they meet and attempt tasks that are challenging, unfamiliar or new. Then talk to them about your experience of learning. Demonstrate how you work around the frustration of not knowing the solution straight away. Record their responses over a series of lessons and use them as your 'pilot' group. At an appropriate time you may wish to share your responses to the training activity at the end of this chapter and provide them with an age and ability appropriate challenge so that they can create and compare similar lists. Post the charts on the wall, where they will highlight some key terminology, serve as an aide memoire for managing emotional responses and demonstrate that learners of all ages have to find ways through the frustrations of learning.

By modelling and actively encouraging a calm and consistent approach to learning in the classroom you will start to develop an environment that is free from stress; allowing the students the security and space they need to access higher order thinking skills.

WATCH OUT FOR...

» Making judgements about students because of their emotional reactions. Keep in mind that your students will be at very different stages in their development of emotional control. It is your responsibility to teach them appropriate and proportionate responses, helping them to understand why persistent displays of raw emotion can be so disruptive to their learning and the concentration of others.

» Expecting students to have instant empathy with your situation. Explaining that you have just come out of a meeting with the Head, have 35 reports to write by Thursday and have an OFSTED inspection next week means very little to year 6. It is more useful to explain that you are feeling snowed under by work and share with them how you plan your time when this happens.

ACTiON POiNTS

Find a quiet space to complete the task below. Give yourself 20 minutes to complete it, in silence and without a break.

Continue the story below. The normal rules of grammar and spelling no longer apply. You must use the writer's 'rules' for spelling, punctuation and grammar.

"lorna said to me, 'You heard the story of
why the dog wont show its eyes?'
I said, 'No, I never'.
She said, 'That's what happens with people on the
way down form what they ben. The storys go'.
She tol me the story then. This is it wrote down the same:

Why the Dog Wont Show Its Eyes
time back way way back befor people got cleavver they had the
1st knowing. They los it when they go the cleverness and now the
cleverness is gone as wel.
Every thing has a shape and so does the nite only you cant see the
shape of note nor you cant think it. If you put your self right you can
know it. Not with knowing in your head but with the 1st knowing.
Where the number creaper grows on the dead stoans and the groun
is sour for 3 days digging the nite stil knows the shape of itself tho
we don't. Some times the nite is the shape of a ear only it anint a
ear we know the shape of. Lissening back for all the souns whatre
gone from us. The hummering of the dead towns and the voyces
befor the towns ben there. Befor the iron ben and fire ben
only littl. Lissening for whats coming as wel.
Time back way way back 1 time it wer Ful of the"

_____

_____

_____

_____

_____

_____

_____

_____

_____

_____

_____

_____

_____

_____

_____

_____

_____

_____

_____

_____

_____

_____

_____

_____

_____

This extract, from "Riddley Walker" is reproduced with kind permission from Bloomsbury Publishing and the author, Russell Hoban.

This task was originally used by Malcolm Reed from Bristol University PGCE English Course.

After completing the task, fill in the chart with
your personal reflections.

MY EMOTIONAL REACTIONS TO THE TASK

_____

_____

_____

_____

_____

HOW i DEALT WiTH THEM

_____

_____

_____

_____

_____

Students who have a reading age lower than that of the resources
you provide have similar, if not stronger emotional responses.
A student who has a reading age more than two years lower than
their age (not at all uncommon) will experience these frustrations
throughout the school day and in most of their classes. Clearly
no-one can comfortably live with the constant challenges this
creates. Students as adults find ways to protect themselves.
They may become withdrawn and avoid work discreetly or,
at the opposite end of the scale, engage in a range of more
disruptive work avoidance techniques.

When I give this task to teachers on training courses the same reactions are displayed. Those who are highly literate and emotionally secure enter into the challenge with enthusiasm. Others seek support from people sitting close by, make paper aeroplanes with the sheet, repeatedly complain about the task and, in one memorable incident, become so angry and frustrated that they walk out of the training space. These reactions are typical of teachers who are successful learners; university educated, academically inclined and experienced professionals.

Keep this in mind when applying the strategies in this handbook and setting expectations for behaviour. My question to teachers is always, 'If these are your reactions to challenging learning situations what should we realistically expect of the students we are challenging?'

CHAPTER 3:
CONSISTENCY AND CERTAINTY

THE PRINCIPLE

Being consistent in dealing with the behaviour of your students means that they know what will happen if they choose to break the rules and equally they know what will happen if they choose to follow the rules. They view you as fair and predictable. When they walk through the door into your classroom they know what to expect there. Moreover they are certain that their behaviour has a direct effect on your responses.

THE PRACTICE

It is not easy to be consistent and it often requires a great deal of emotional control. Inconsistency, at best, results in your students being wary of you and, at worst, leads to resentment and confrontation. Becoming agitated by the fifth latecomer who interrupts the introduction to your lesson and sending them outside the moment they open the door relieves your tension briefly but sends confusing messages to the rest of the class. 'Fairness' is a very important concept to your students and persistent inconsistencies in your behaviour can damage relationships. It is hard work trying to remain consistent and fair all of the time. When you next reflect on an incident and decide that your actions were not consistent...

>> **Meet the student when you both have time to talk**
>> **Apologise for your inconsistency**
>> **Explain that your goal is to be fair and consistent and you will be open about mistakes**
>> **Thank the student for being patient with you**
>> **Record the development of the relationship from this point onwards**

I remember being unfairly harsh on a Year 11 class who met me for the first time and was still grieving the loss of their previous teacher. It was a difficult lesson fuelled by emotional energy on both sides and I was inconsistent, unfair and angry. I left the lesson worried that I had blown it. I reflected that I could not ignore my own behaviour when I met them again and needed to address it with them. I opened the following lesson by apologising for my behaviour and being as honest as I could about how I felt. They listened intently and without comment. The mood in the room eased and the lesson was calmer and more productive. The foundations for our relationship had been set. Later in the year the same class commented that they had been shocked by my willingness to apologise and that their worries about me had been diffused.

When you hear students talking about their teachers they discuss those who are consistent, ('Don't mess about in her lesson, she always gets you,') and those who are not, ('I hate him, he send me out for nothing, I only asked a question' **(sic))**. They also recognise those teachers who use praise more than sanctions ('She never shouts, she's really nice, I can just get on with my work'). They know when you are late to the lesson, unprepared, impatient or react with more emotion than thought. They are forming opinions about your consistency that are quickly set and hard to change. They bring these attitudes and expectations to your classroom and begin the class with them. Lessons can feel like an uphill struggle when students expect to be treated unfairly or lack a consistent model. The more they sense inconsistency the more they will be tempted to exploit it or defend against it and the classroom becomes an unstable place for learning.

In order for your students to be clear about which consequences (positive and negative) follow certain actions, you need to display your responses to explicit behaviour clearly. The more consistent you are with applying these consequences, the more the students will become 'certain' that poor choices will result in sanctions and good choices in rewards. This can take some time so you need to be dogged in your persistence. If you place a heavy focus on praise and rewards, you will have a better chance of success and the pace of change will be accelerated.

WATCH OUT FOR...

» Judging yourself too harshly. We need to be consistent but we are not mechanoids. There are days when we feel shaky, tired, irritated and like running for the nearest beach. Days when Colin's persistent whispering seems designed as a slow torture. Days when, despite our best efforts, we deliver an unfair consequence or act out of character. Don't beat yourself up over these occasional lapses. Remember that you are the adult, the professional, and it is your responsibility to control the urge to throttle. Take a step back and use the techniques that work. Aim for 7 out of 10 and be satisfied with achieving the 7.

» Worrying about giving out too many rewards and/or sanctions. At first the students will test the system. You may find yourself flooded by requests for rewards and/or spending a great deal of time giving and chasing up sanctions. Expect this stage in the introduction of new boundaries (positive and negative). When the students feel the system (does 'it' need specifying?) has been sufficiently tested and they can predict your responses accurately, things will level out. It is not unusual for groups of students to repeatedly reach the most serious sanctions in the first few weeks. Do not be put off by this, stay consistent and students' choices will change.

ACTION POINTS

List the most frequent positive and negative behaviour
students exhibit in your classroom.

POSITIVE BEHAVIOUR

_____

_____

_____

_____

_____

_____

NEGATIVE BEHAVIOUR

_____

_____

_____

_____

_____

_____

Decide on the two or three rules that will operate in your classroom.
They should be ones that cover as many of the above examples of
behaviour as possible. Don't be tempted to negotiate these rules with
the students yet. You may want to when you have developed stronger
relationships, but for now you are the teacher, it is your classroom
and you get to decide on what the rules are.

If you use the Learning Rituals as described in the next chapter then 'Follow the Learning Ritual' should be your first rule. In time you may want all activities to fall within these rituals but to start with you may find it useful to choose **two or three** further rules. The examples below may help:

» **When someone is talking, listen, or, one voice only**
» **Stay 'on task'**
» **Bring the correct equipment to the lesson (including homework)**
» **Do not disturb others who are working**
» **Stay in your working area**
» **No swearing or offensive language**
» **Follow the teacher's instructions straight away**

RULES

1.   Follow the Learning Ritual _____

_____

_____

_____

I find frameworks for applying rules, rewards and sanctions that use graduated sanctions, easier to work with. One alternative to this is a points system where all students begin a new term or half term with, say, 20 points. Different challenging behaviour attracts tariffs and staff remove points from the students' total. My experience with these models is they can:

» **encourage confrontation when applying sanctions as you are taking points away from the student, and their focus on rewards can easily be lost**
» **create an opportunity for a student to lose all of their 'chances' in one day**
» **be more open to abuse by angry teachers:
'Right, that's another 5 points off'**

With a graduated rewards and sanctions system there are no points and everyone starts with a blank sheet every lesson. Students can clearly see what reward or sanction comes next and can make decisions accordingly.

Decide what sanctions will appear on your graduated list for students who choose not to follow the rules. You should make it clear to students that if there is a serious incident, such as violent or dangerous behaviour or verbal abuse directed at the teacher, you will not use warnings or other graduated sanctions but take immediate steps to remove the student or call for support.

You can choose to have one or two verbal warnings before more serious sanctions are applied. Be explicit with your language when phrasing your rules. Avoid loaded phrases such as 'respect' or 'manners'. Use the 'Popular Sanctions' lists for ideas. Each time a rule is broken the severity of the sanction should increase.

GRADUATED SANCTIONS

1st	Verbal warning
2nd	
3rd	
4th	
5th	
6th	

Now work out an appropriate scale of rewards. Again there is a list of ideas to get you started. Rewards should be desirable, age appropriate and easily organised. You may choose to have different rewards lists for different classes.

GRADUATED REWARDS

1st	Verbal praise
2nd	
3rd	
4th	
5th	
6th	

Display this chart on the walls of your teaching space and explain it to the students. Use and keep to the rewards and sanctions you have listed. Don't deviate from the plan. When you catch a student following the rules, reward them; when you see them breaking the rules warn them and then deliver sanctions. At the end of the first week review the chart and explain any changes to the students. Be prepared for students to challenge rules, rewards or sanctions that don't appear on the chart; they will help to keep your responses consistent.

POPULAR REWARDS

POSITIVE NOTES HOME

Type up photocopy sheets of A5 or A6 with:
'Dear Parent/Guardian, Just a quick note to say how pleased I am with ....'s work in class today .etc.'
Keep a stack on your desk and use them as a higher order reward. Students will value these notes more than you might imagine. I had a Year 11 girl who still used one I gave her in Year 8 to wave at her parents when they questioned her school/social life balance.

HOMEWORK PASS/EXTENSION

This is a token given and signed by the teacher to allow the student permission not to do the homework or hand it in late as appropriate.

POSITIVE REFERRAL

Send a student, either during the lesson or at an appropriate time, to see a colleague for further acknowledgement and praise.

MERITS/STICKERS/STAR CHARTS

If your school does not already have a policy, or has one that is solely related to learning, you need to create a cumulative rewards system with tangible rewards at, say, 15, 50 & 100 points to support good choices in behaviour. Record merits in students' individual exercise books or homework diaries. Use an ink stamp or sheets of stickers or bits of paper with your signature and keep a record yourself.

CLASS REWARDS

Post a sheet of A4 paper on the wall with a tally chart entitled 'Class Reward'. Any student can earn a class reward point and once earned they cannot be taken away. Once the class reaches 20/40/60 points the class earns a reward. Differentiate the target total to keep your classes motivated; the class that struggles to begin the lesson will need a shorter-term target than the one you can already get working. Make the rewards age appropriate and desirable. For instance they might be able to listen to music while they work, work outside in the summer, have extended story time. You may choose to negotiate these rewards in time and ask them what they think appropriate rewards (that don't involve money!) might be.

'LEAVE FiRST' TOKEN

Very useful if you have the students before break, lunch or at the end of the day.

SUBJECT/CLASS AWARD CERTiFiCATE

Use as a higher order reward and send a copy direct to the parents/guardians.

CHOOSiNG WHERE TO SiT

Earning the right to negotiate over their place on the seating plan.

POPULAR SANCTIONS

IMPOSITIONS

Students are given additional work to complete at home that, when completed, is signed by their parent/guardian. Type up the instructions for the task and have five or six different ones photocopied so that you have them ready. Make a note at the bottom of the imposition explaining the consequence of not handing the work in before school the following day. The work should be linked to their work in class, relevant, appropriate and differentiated to take half an hour of the student's time. Do not give lines or repetitive tasks as these are completed with resentment rather than thought.

LUNCHTIME DETENTION

I have never been keen on detention as a sanction unless I have an opportunity to discuss the students' choices with them. After school detentions are difficult to enforce, cause complications with the timings of families and eat into students' life out of school. Lunchtime detentions are easier to enforce and students tend to resent them less. Keep the detention to 15 minutes since a longer punishment does not have more positive impact, and find an opportunity to build your professional relationship with the student.

A MOMENT AFTER CLASS

Hold the student back after class very briefly to discuss their poor choices. You are showing them that you care about the choices they make in your lesson.

CLASS REPORT

Keep a brief record of the student's behaviour in each lesson over an agreed period. Explain that when it is complete a copy will be sent to the Parents, Deputy Head etc. At the end of each lesson read the comment to the student and ask them to co-sign the report. Be prepared to reward better choices. In individual lessons apply your rules and rituals to students on report in the same way as others.

TiME OUT

Give time outside the classroom, ideally supervised by another colleague, to allow the student a few minutes to calm down and rejoin the lesson. The language is important here. A 'time out' is less aggressive than being 'sent out' and echoes 'time out' in sport where players are given time to calm down away from the field of play.

PHONE CALL HOME

An effective sanction but one that must be handled with care. Take advice from a senior colleague about the home situation and likely impact of the call; many parents use corporal punishment and this association may not be desirable. Think carefully about the time that you call and prepare what you are going to say and how you are going to leave the conversation.

MOViNG A STUDENT (TO SiT ELSEWHERE iN THE ROOM)

It is important that when a student reaches this sanction it is delivered privately, preferably away from other students. If the interaction is too public you risk involving others and causing humiliation.

'PARKiNG'

Gentler terminology for moving the student out of the classroom to sit with or 'be parked' with another teacher who is teaching another class. Make prior arrangements with a senior colleague so you can send the student with his work. Give the student a prepared note or laminated card to take with him. Have a look at your school policy as it may determine what happens to students who have to be removed from the lesson.

CHAPTER 4:
LEARNING RITUALS

THE PRINCIPLE

Students need to have your expectations for learning clearly explained and posted on the walls of the classroom. Do not assume that they know how to behave in the classroom, regardless of their age, but teach them the precise rules for each task. Good Early Years teaching is a strong model here as teachers of this age group spend a great deal of time initiating and negotiating learning rituals. When the rules for each type of activity (e.g. sitting on the carpet and listening, working in groups, quiet individual study, going outside to play) are clear to everyone, students can then choose to follow these rules and receive rewards, or not to follow them and receive a warning followed by sanctions.

THE PRACTICE

Break down each different learning ritual into what is expected at each stage. Spend time teaching this to the class and involve them in creating attractive displays in the room on large chart paper. Phrase your rules positively, avoid use of 'do not' and 'no', avoid absolutes like 'silence' and value-loaded phrases such as 'polite' or 'respect'. At each stage describe the desired behaviour, e.g. 'When someone is speaking, listen' or, 'Look at me'.

Teach the new rituals immediately before the task, giving examples and modelling your responses carefully. When the task is revisited it is vital that you run over the routine with the students. When the activity begins, focus on those students who are following the rules and use praise and positive reinforcement to support their good choices; 'Thank you, this table, you have stopped your conversations, got your pens out and are listening. That is number two on our agreement, well done.' When students choose to break the rules, give a clear, private verbal warning, 'You have chosen not to follow the third part of our learning ritual. I am giving you a verbal warning.

I need you to follow the agreed plan. I will come back in a while and will be looking to praise better choices'. If the rule break is repeated, apply sanctions. Indicate on the displays which rule has been kept/broken to reinforce the ritual. Introduce only one new routine at a time and teach it until the students know it without looking at the display.

A good technique for getting the attention of the whole class is to use a 'countdown' from 5 or 10 to allow students the time to finish their conversations or work and listen to the next instruction. Explain to the class that you are using countdown to give them fair warning that they need to listen and that it is far more polite than calling for immediate silence. Embellish your countdown with clear instructions so that students know what is expected and be prepared to modify it for different groups:

- » **'Five, you should be finishing the sentence that you are writing**
- » **Four, turn to look at the board**
- » **Three, excellent Marcus, a merit for being the first to give me your full attention**
- » **Two, quickly back to your place**
- » **One, all pens and pencils down now**
- » **Half, all looking this way**
- » **Zero, thank you.'**

Some students may join in the countdown with you at first, some will not be quiet by the time you get to zero but persevere, use praise and rewards techniques described in this book to reinforce its importance and it can become an extremely efficient tool for those times when you need everyone's attention. You may already have a technique for getting everyone's attention, e.g. hands up. The countdown technique is more effective as it is time related and does not rely on students seeing you.

WATCH OUT FOR...

>> Displaying the rules, but discreetly and/or in only one area of the classroom. Think about where your rules are best displayed. A checklist of rules for entering and leaving the classroom should be on the door of the room. Similarly, the rules for individual work at tables need to be visible to everyone as they work.

>> Enthusiastically introducing rituals and then not referring to them again until sanctions need to be applied. Use the rituals to support your discussions with students. Point to and refer to them tirelessly until the students realise that you are not going to be diverted from them.

>> Establishing too many new rituals too soon. Introduce new rituals gradually and over time. Allow one or two to become embedded in the learning before developing more advanced rituals, such as moving furniture around or class discussion. Too many new rituals too soon are confusing for both teacher and students.

ACTION POINTS

Create a ritual for entering the classroom and list five observable behaviours that you wish to see from all students. Write them in the chart.

Learning Ritual for Entering the Classroom

1.
2.
3.
4.
5.

Integrating latecomers into the lesson can be very disruptive and time consuming. Using a ritual for latecomers will not stop all students arriving late but it will help them to check their behaviour and help you to control their arrival so that it causes least disturbance to the class.

What do you want students who arrive late to do? Wait outside and knock? Take the seat nearest the door? See you at the end of the lesson? Wait for an opportunity to join in with the lesson? Go to their seat and get their equipment ready for the lesson? Speak to you immediately on arrival? Sign a late register? Walk in quietly without speaking to other students?

Ritual for Arriving Late

1. _____

2. _____

3. _____

4. _____

5. _____

Post the two rituals on the outside of the door to your classroom so they can be clearly seen by all classes as they arrive at your lesson. Teach the class these rituals step by step, modelling the desired behaviours. Encourage their use with positive reinforcement and praise in the first instance and sanctions when necessary. When the class know these well, think about other rituals that you would like students to use and understand: moving around the room, leaving the room, group discussion, peer assessment.

CHAPTER 5: LANGUAGE

THE PRINCIPLE

In 'Language and Learning' James Britton makes it clear that language is a map through which humans construct their view of the world. (James Britton, 'Language and Learning') Tell a child that he is 'naughty' or 'a trouble maker' and he will include it in his map. Repeat that language often enough and he will route everything through it. Through careful use of language you can help students to make better choices about their behaviour and understand the route to success in their learning.

The language you use can help to diffuse potential problems in the classroom, protect and enhance students' views of themselves and depersonalise challenges to their actions. The vocabulary that you use with the students is more controlled when it has been thought through and planned. Relying on improvisation is unreliable and inconsistent.

THE PRACTICE

As a teacher you are often performing. You may not feel confident, assertive or positive on a Monday morning but you strive to give your students this impression. Perceived weaknesses in your use of language and tone of voice often lead to instructions being ignored or rejected immediately, '**Please** take your coat off, I am too tired to deal with you today', or, 'If you are not going to listen to me I cannot teach you'. Making careful choices in your use of language, maintaining a consistent tone of voice and confident intonation means that you can communicate assertively even in a weakened emotional state. This takes some discipline on your part. You need to maintain an assertive performance even when you become weary of the constant interruptions and your emotional brain tempts you into pleading with the students or throwing your hands up and slumping into your chair. Some of the key words and phrases suggested here can help you develop an assertive vocabulary and tone.

'Choice' is an important concept in behaviour management. When students know the rules, rituals and expectations explicitly, then they can make a choice whether to follow them or not. All human beings make choices about their behaviour throughout the day. As a teacher you are trying to teach students to make better choices about their behaviour. Using the word 'choice' allows you to attack the choice and not the student. It puts the responsibility for behaviour on to the student, encourages discussion that is about his choice and not his personality and focuses attention on his choices and not the behaviour of others. It de-personalises the interaction. Discuss a student's 'poor choices' and 'good choices' in his behaviour, e.g. 'You made some poor choices in your behaviour today, particularly the standing on the chair and throwing your pen down. In tomorrow's lesson I need you to make better choices. I remember last week when you helped me to clear up, that was a good choice.' Help students to learn that all choices have consequences. Present choices to students, 'You can continue listening to your walkman and then have it confiscated, or you can put it away and carry on with your work. It's your choice'.

If students want to argue about sanctions or discuss rewards explain that you will not discuss them in 'learning time' but can find time outside the lesson to do so. You may then have more time to provide more detailed questioning to help the student understand his own choices. For example, 'What do you think the poor choices were that caught my attention?' and 'What do you think you could do to avoid this happening in the next lesson?'

'Certainty' is an important word and concept for your students. Use it when you teach your rules and rituals. 'If you make good choices you can be certain that I will recognise them and reward them. The same goes for poor choices. You can be certain that sanctions will follow and I will work as hard as I can to make this happen'.

All students, but especially those who have had a string of supply teachers or an unreliable home life, need to hear that you 'care' about them, their work and behaviour. As a class teacher I often used the phrase, 'I'm here for the long term, I care about your behaviour and am going to work with you to help you succeed'. When you apply a sanction it can be softened by explaining that you 'care about his success too much to allow poor choices to stop his learning'.

Your physical language is read (and misread) by students all the time. Check that you are modelling appropriate body language for a learning space.

AVOID

>> **Pointing at students with your finger, or at the door, 'Get out!' etc**
>> **Rolling your eyes**
>> **Turning your back on students who are talking to you**
>> **Standing over students**
>> **Invading their personal space too quickly and without invitation**
>> **Demanding sustained eye contact**
   (an aggressive act in many cultures)
>> **Using any form of aggressive touch**
>> **Dismissive hand gestures**
>> **Aggressive tensing of the facial muscles particularly eyebrows**
>> **Using your size to physically dominate an interaction**

INSTEAD USE

>> **Use your whole hand to gesticulate rather in preference to a finger**
>> **Questioning and open faces**
>> **Stepping back from a difficult conversation to regroup**
>> **Slow approach to a student's working space**
>> **Eye level conversations**

WATCH OUT FOR

» Slipping back to the terminology that you have always used when lessons become stressful and your emotional brain takes over. Practise using new vocabulary and phrases as you are going to work so that they become a natural part of the language you are modelling.

» Sending mixed messages to students by contrasting verbal and physical language, e.g. smiling when applying sanctions or giving a reward without establishing gentle eye contact.

ACTION POINTS

Complete the exercise comparing the language that you have grown up with, the language you have used in the past and the language you could use now. Start introducing the new vocabulary this week, so that by the end of the week you have weeded out the vocabulary that is not supporting your students' behaviour. Think carefully about where the language that you have always used has come from, your own teachers, parents, colleagues, and question it hard.

INCIDENT – THROWING A PIECE OF PAPER ACROSS THE ROOM

What might your teachers have said to you?

"_____"

What would you usually say to a student?

"_____"

And now?

"_____"

INCIDENT – SHOUTING OUT IN CLASS

What might your teachers have said to you?

"_____"

What would you usually say to a student

"_____"

And now?

"_____"

INCIDENT – REFUSING TO FOLLOW INSTRUCTIONS

What might your teachers have said to you?

"_____"

What would you usually say to a student?

"_____"

And now?

"_____"

CHAPTER 6:
PRAISE AND REWARD

THE PRINCIPLE

Human beings are motivated by acknowledgement of their work, praise and reward. In the classroom, praise is the most powerful tool you have for managing the behaviour of your students. If you positively reinforce the behaviour that you want and expect, students will respond by seeking your attention though fair means rather than foul. Praise changes relationships, raises self-esteem, increases motivation and improves attitudes to teacher, subject and school.

THE PRACTICE

You need to acknowledge students who are following your instructions and rituals with a 'thank you' or non verbal sign (thumbs up, nod of the head) coupled with eye contact. This is a positive reinforcement of their behaviour, good manners and an important step to creating a positive culture in the classroom. I cannot imagine training a roomful of adults without saying thank you; the same follows for students.

You need to be intelligent with your use of praise as it has differing effects on individuals. Not all human beings want public praise; in fact many find it as distressing as public admonishment. Hold up the work from a student as an example to the rest of the class and a broad smile may open up on the face of one pupil, but for another it is humiliating, unwelcome and may discourage him from aiming for similar standards in the future.

Students appreciate praise when it is delivered discreetly, privately and fairly. They need to know that your praise is sincere and deserved. They need praise that is individualised, and as a teacher you need to be prepared to deliver this using your own language and style; repeating 'praise phrases' will not convince anyone that you truly appreciate their work and ability to stay within the rules. Get down to a student's eye level by crouching next to his working table. Tell him what you are praising and why and use physical and verbal language that you are comfortable with.

Don't reserve your acknowledgement and praise for only the best behaved students. Praise those students who quietly get on with their work, those who find progress difficult and those whose concentration drifts. Differentiate your praise; the student who struggles with written work yet completes the opening paragraph may deserve equal praise to the literate student presenting a finished story. Change your own perspective to 'catch someone doing the right thing'. The accomplished Year One teacher who brings her class to order by focusing on the students who are following the rules is a strong example here ('Just look at Samuel, he is sitting up straight with his table tidy ready to leave for lunch. Well done Samuel, you can go first'). Use positive reinforcement and acknowledgement to draw other students back on task without drawing attention to them; the 'off task' student may well be drawn back to work by your attention to the hard work of his neighbour. It is a gentler and less intrusive first step sending the message, but not confronting the behaviour immediately.

Praise students as they are leaving the room; 'Thank you for your hard work today Ayesha, you have really impressed me with your concentration'.

There has been great debate in recent years about touch. I have always tried to help students understand that touch is a human response; not necessarily violent or sexual but encouraging, affirming and a part of human communication. For students that you have spent time getting to know and trust, a 'safe touch' on the shoulder or upper arm is not going to be misunderstood. Obviously for classes with whom you have not built a relationship, touch should not be a first step. In many secondary schools there is great fear about touch. I understand the reservations, the scare stories and the knee jerk advice given on touch. But what are we teaching students if we work with them every day yet refuse to touch them regardless of the situation? In early years or primary contexts there is no choice – just try comforting a distressed four year old without giving him a cuddle.

WATCH OUT FOR...

>> Using all of your positive energy on the first day. Being positive and delivering praise consistently and fairly throughout your working day can be exhausting. Praise is hard work at first, especially at the end of a long day with a challenging group, but it pays dividends in the short, long and medium term.

>> Taking away praise/rewards. The students need to know that your praise is not conditional on their continued good behaviour. If you give students sincere praise and perhaps a reward for their hard work it cannot be revoked. If they make poor choices afterwards give a verbal warning and then apply sanctions. There is no conflict in students receiving both.

>> Overusing praise, as it will become meaningless to the students. Save your most enthusiastic praise for students who deserve it most.

» Slipping back into negatives when praise doesn't work the first time. Your students need to be convinced that your classroom is a consistently positive environment. This cannot be achieved in one day and your positive responses will need to become part of your teaching style and not an afterthought.

» Passing over those students who work quietly and consistently throughout your lessons. They deserve and need your acknowledgement and praise. Without it they may choose to gain attention by less positive means. Stand by the door as the students leave and catch those students you may have missed in the lesson.

ACTION POINTS

In the first week use the tally chart to record the positive and negative comments that you give to the class (ask a support teacher or observing colleague to help if appropriate). Aim for a ratio of 5:1 positive to negative comments. Try to phrase a negative reaction in positive terms. For example. 'Thank you for sitting down so quickly, you will need the hand that is in Oliver's bag to write down the first key word' as opposed to, 'Stop doing that, you are supposed to be listening to me, how many times have I told you...' After the lesson note down any words or phrases that had a positive impact and those that you wish you hadn't said.

POSiTiVE COMMENTS

Tally total _____

WORDS/PHRASES TO WATCH OUT FOR

_____
_____
_____
_____
_____
_____
_____
_____
_____

NEGATiVE COMMENTS

Tally total _____

WORDS/PHRASES TO WATCH OUT FOR

_____
_____
_____
_____
_____
_____
_____
_____
_____

CHAPTER 7:
SANCTIONS:
WHEN STUDENTS BREAK THE RULES

THE PRINCIPLE

Your sanctions must be graduated, applied consistently and gently and leave the students' self esteem intact. Students need to be spoken to privately whenever possible, your approach should be non-threatening, with the discussion at eye level. Sanctions must attack the behaviour choice and not the child. When students choose to break rules that have been taught and made explicit through displays on the classroom walls, sanctions need to be applied.

THE PRACTICE

Don't be surprised when students break your rules and rituals. Expect it, plan for it and use it as an opportunity to teach them about better choices.

There are many non-verbal ways in which you can communicate with the students about their choices before approaching them and intervening. Your non-verbal cues may not be immediately or accurately understood by a new group of students and you may need to be explicit about the techniques that you are using. For example, 'When I am speaking to the class and I stand next to your table I am giving you a chance to check your choices before I need to stop and give you a verbal warning'. When the class can read your non-verbal cues, your initial response can be discreet yet still effective. You can begin to manage minor infringements without being interrupted or having to stop what you are saying to the class.

TRY THESE:

>> **Standing or sitting next to the student;**
   it will encourage them to check their behaviour.

>> **Gaining eye contact that gently says, 'Come on,**
   let's get back to work'.

>> **Using agreed signals such as holding up four fingers to**
   ask them to place four legs of the chair on the floor.

>> **Indicating their chair with an open palm to invite them to sit down.**

>> **Standing next to the charts that display the learning rituals**
   and rules and combining eye contact with a finger on
   the chart sends a clear message.

Over time you will be able to build up a range of non-verbal cues that allow students' poor choices to be addressed subtly within the 'flow' of your teaching.

Unless it is a serious incident, e.g. verbal abuse directed at the teacher, violent behaviour endangering the class, your first sanction should be a verbal warning. Take a moment to prepare what you are going to say to the student. Approach the student calmly and gently and get down to their eye level. Explain that the behaviour witnessed is contrary to the rules and that you are giving them a warning. Then focus on the learning that you expect to see the student engaged in.

If the student tries to divert the conversation or bring in the behaviour of another student use, you can say, 'I understand what you are saying but we are talking about...' or, 'I hear that but I am talking about your choices'. You are acknowledging his conversation but returning the focus back to the undesirable behaviour. Finish your discussion by referring to the student's previous good behaviour, 'Last lesson you worked really hard on this, try and get back to where you were' and leave them feeling positive about the rest of the lesson.

You may even feign surprise at his poor choices, 'You are not someone who usually makes poor choices...' Then walk away. Turn your attention to the rest of the class and catch someone doing the right thing. Give the student the space to calm down, consider his next choice and act upon it. After a couple of minutes check that the student who received the sanction is back on task and give him a gentle 'thank you'. If he is still choosing to break the rules return and apply your second sanction, usually a request for him to see you after class to discuss his behaviour choices.

WATCH OUT FOR...

» 'Hovering' by a student after you have applied a sanction. The student needs time and space to make better choices about her behaviour and your continued proximity makes this very difficult. I have observed teachers who have a graduated sanctions list and by standing over a student, manage to apply all five sanctions in 30 seconds. The student feels humiliated and resentful. His personal space has been invaded and he has not been given a fair chance to change his behaviour. A small rules break suddenly escalates into a full-blown confrontation that does not meet the needs of the student and teacher.

» Holding grudges. Each lesson should be a clean sheet for students. Poor choices in the previous lesson should either be dealt with in the interim or at another time. Students need to know that they have not been labelled by their previous poor choices.

» Giving a sanction and then taking it away. Regardless of how many good choices the student makes after a sanction is applied you should not remove the sanction. Your students need to understand that there are consequences to certain choices and these are not negotiable. You should reward good choices even if they follow poor ones. It is not unusual for some students to leave the classroom with both.

ACTION POINTS

Read the sample structure for intervention and fill in the gaps with examples using vocabulary you are comfortable with. Learn and practise the structure for applying the sanctions below until you are comfortable with the sequence. Don't leave out section 'c' as the strongest model for the behaviour that you expect is the students' previous good choices. This structure is also extremely useful when delivering praise, (I have included it in italics). In both instances you need to have a structure for opening, developing and closing the interaction efficiently, leaving both parties with their self-esteem intact.

SAMPLE STRUCTURE FOR iNTERVENTiON

Delivering warning/sanction

Delivering praise

a. Gentle approach, personal, non threatening, eye level, eye contact.

b. State the behaviour that was observed and which ritual/rule it contravenes.

b. *State exactly what it is that you are praising and why.*

Example: _____

c. Tell the student what the sanction is. Refer to previous good behaviour/learning as a model for desired behaviour.

c. *Tell the student what the reward is.*

Example: _____

d. Tell the student what will happen if he continues with this approach to learning.

Example: _____

e. Tell him that his choice was poor and he needs to make better choices.

e. *Thank him for making the right choices.*

Example: _____

f. Walk away from the student; allow him time to make a better choice. If he is back 'on task' give him appropriate praise and/or acknowledgement.

g. Scan the room and catch somebody following the routine.

Do not discuss consequences in learning time.
Use 'I understand' or 'I hear what you are saying' and return to you original point.

Do not allow yourself to be drawn away from the conversation you want to have.

Recognise secondary behaviours and avoid 'chasing' them (see Chapter 12 managing Confrontation)

CHAPTER 8:
MANAGING CONFRONTATION
AND STOPPING IT FROM ESCALATING

THE PRINCIPLE

There will be times when, regardless of how well you structure your application of sanctions, you find yourself in a confrontation with a student. There will also be times when you are confronted by a student, without warning, for no explicit reason.

The way you manage the confrontation has a direct affect on its outcome; even if the outcome is not an instant solution. A carefully managed confrontation with a student can have positive outcomes even if the beginning of the conversation was a difficult experience for both parties. At all times remember who the adult is, model the behaviour you expect and enjoy skilfully managing the situation to meet the best needs of your students.

THE PRACTICE

Confrontations can happen in an instant and often when you are least expecting them. You need to work to keep your own emotions in check throughout, to protect yourself and the student. Try to view the confrontation for what it really is, an adult modelling and teaching a child about expected behaviour. I have had many weekends tarnished by guilt after saying the wrong thing to the wrong student late on a Friday afternoon.

Your response to the first signs of a confrontation sets the rhythm of the rest of the discussion. Change your focus from being the speaker to being the listener. While you are listening look at your own body language and soften it, take a step back, lower your hands, indicate with open palms rather than pointed fingers, remove any aggressive tightening of the facial muscles and then prepare what you are going to say.

We usually know what our opening sentence will be but few plan beyond it. Work through what you are going to say in response, how you will say it and how you are going to end the conversation, and keep it on track. As with applying sanctions, students need to know that they are being listened to. Use, 'I hear what you are saying' and, 'I understand'. You will find that the confrontation needs the fuel of an equally confrontational response to keep it escalating. If your response is to listen, and keep listening until the student has finished and take immediate steps to de-escalate, using appropriate physical and verbal language, any aggression will be short lived. Don't try to solve all confrontations instantly. You may need to walk away and take time and advice on how to resolve the situation. You may need to listen, record and then refer on to a senior colleague. When students have sworn, threatened and physically confronted me, I never improved the situation through an aggressive or emotional response.

Some students enjoy a confrontation with a teacher. It can be an opportunity for adrenaline-fuelled interlude into his otherwise uneventful day and is quickly forgotten. For others it is frightening and shocking. It can damage the teacher/student relationship irrevocably. Your careful management of confrontation can quell the former and protect the latter.

As soon as possible after the incident make a detailed chronological written record of what happened and who said what. This is not only a useful reflective (and cathartic) action but also clarifies the incident for senior colleagues and parents. If appropriate, encourage the student to do the same and call it a 'Think Sheet' with key questions 'What happened to make you feel wound up? What did you do about this? What do you think that you should do next time? Use a cold comparison of the two to learn more about the effect of your actions and reactions on the student.

WATCH OUT FOR...

» Chasing secondary behaviours. Students, like teachers, have a sophisticated armoury to defend themselves when confronted. A secondary behaviour might be the smirk that glides across the face of a student who is supposed to be looking ashamed, or the chair that is pushed back too hard after the student is sent from the room. These behaviours can attract a stronger response than the initial incident. They are 'chase me' behaviours designed to get an emotional response from the teacher. Don't ignore them but choose the right time to address them when the student has calmed down.

» Allowing the discussion to be diverted. There are common diversionary tactics that can extend a ten second confrontation into an hour-long discussion. They usually start with, 'I don't like this class and my Dad says it's a waste of time anyway' or, 'What's the point of History anyway?' Use, 'I understand but...' or, 'I hear what you are saying but...' to get the conversation back on track.

» Bringing up past misdemeanours or using as a model the example of siblings or other students 'Your brother never behaved like this'

» Invading students' personal space. Students may feel threatened and become aggressive if their personal space is continually violated

» Making accusations. Use questions instead 'Nathan, are you ready to begin?' rather than 'Nathan, put that magazine away'.

» Offering unsolicited advice or criticism when discussing choices with students.

ACTION POINTS

Plan your responses to confrontation using the chart. Refer to them throughout the week, adopting them where appropriate. Measure the students' reaction to them carefully.

Your first reaction to an escalating confrontation

_____

While the student is speaking you will:

_____

When you want to exit the confrontation you will say:
"_____"

As soon as the confrontation has finished you will

_____

When sufficient time has elapsed you will

_____

CHAPTER 9: SEEKING SUPPORT: YOUR CLASSROOM, YOUR RESPONSIBILITY

THE PRINCIPLE

As a teacher, the students in your class are your responsibility. You alone are responsible for managing their behaviour in your classroom. It is your right to seek support from senior staff and parents when necessary, but you need to manage this support carefully. If you delegate responsibility to a colleague entirely it will weaken your relationship with the student and the class. You have a responsibility to remain a part of the management of even the most challenging students, even if that student has been removed from the class and is being dealt with by someone else.

THE PRACTICE

It goes something like this...A student behaves appallingly in class and a senior manager is called for. With your temper only just in check, you explain what has happened and the student is taken away to receive appropriate punishment. You return to your classroom, satisfied that the student has been disciplined, and try to calm yourself and the rest of the class down. The next time you see this student is at the start of your next lesson together. The student enters holding a report card and refuses to engage with you or the lesson. Another incident occurs and the senior colleague is summoned and again removes the student. You complain that nothing has changed and the support you have received is not solving anything. You even start to believe that the student in question is 'unteachable' and there is a general grunt of agreement beneath mugs of tea in the staff room. The student clearly resents the way that he has been treated and most of his resentment is directed at you.

If you call for support during a lesson, speak to the colleague privately and discreetly, preferably away from the student in question. If the student is removed from the lesson make time before the next lesson with the same class to speak to the student calmly and quietly, preferably with the supporting colleague in the meeting. This meeting is vital. Make the time to do it and the investment will pay off. Don't be put off by the number of other incidents the student may have been involved in that day. Your primary concern should be the student's behaviour in **your** class.

By meeting with him, calmly explaining why he had to be removed and what behaviour you expect to see from him next time, you are sending a clear message to the student; you want him to be a part of the class, you care about his learning and you are responsible for the behaviour of all students in your class. This message may not filter through in the first instance but over time it will become clear. You will feel involved in his reintegration and your relationship with him will develop. You will be able to refer to the conversation you have had in future incidents and the class will begin to understand that you use support from other colleagues as a temporary measure and not as a permanent attempt at a solution.

Most students prefer to separate their home life from their life in school. They are often keen to avoid direct discussion between parents and teachers; I remember as a student the anxiety the build up to parents' evenings elicited. Knowing that all of my sins would be laid bare and I would have to confront them in front of my teachers and parents was not a comfortable experience. Try to establish individual rapport with parents so they know who they are dealing with, they can put a face to a name and over time build up trust in their child's teacher. Find regular opportunities to communicate with parents about the child's progress. Don't wait for the parent to come to you at parents' evenings but go over and introduce yourself.

Give regular feedback if a child is on subject report, send a note home, or pick up the phone, 'Just giving you a quick call to let you know how Joshua is getting on...'. When there is a bond between home and school the child will see that his behaviour and its consequences are not confined to the classroom. The relationships I built up with parents were one of the most effective behaviour management tools I could draw on. I would often phone home before the student arrived there or on some memorable occasions be sitting drinking tea with the parent when the child arrived home from school. Once the child knows that a positive relationship exists and that consistent and regular contact is maintained he will check his behaviour carefully and modify responses accordingly.

WATCH OUT FOR....

>> Deferring responsibility to senior mangers too quickly, too often or too publicly, 'When your Year Head hears about this...' or, 'I'm going straight to the Head'.

>> The student who has been excluded from school after an incident in your lesson. His feelings of resentment are likely to be stronger and he will have had a greater input form senior colleagues and parents. Ask to be a part of the reintegration process and the negotiations with the student even if the exclusion is bundled with other incidents.

>> Avoid labelling students (publicly or privately) with negative expectations. It will colour your responses to these students and prevent them from changing their responses to your classroom management.

>> Only seeking support for negative behaviours. Forewarn and negotiate with senior colleagues so that you can send students to them for praise or ask them to drop into your lesson to deliver praise. Focus particularly on those students who, having made poor choices, then make a decision to work hard.

ACTION POINTS

Photocopy the chart and either attach it to your school's incident report sheet or use it as a stand alone. When an incident occurs that requires the support of a senior colleague, hand the checklist to them so that they can see the strategies that you have used with this student. This checklist is useful as an aide memoire for yourself and a prompt sheet when discussing the incident with the student after the lesson. It also serves to remind senior colleagues that you are using positive behaviour management techniques and places the responsibility for the incident firmly with the student.

BEHAVIOUR MANAGEMENT STRATEGIES USED

	TICK
Acknowledged good behaviour choices	☐
Spoke to the student privately and on eye level	☐
Was consistent in application of classroom behaviour plan	☐
Gave the student time and space to rectify behaviour	☐
Listened to the student	☐
Referred to the learning rituals (posted on the wall)	☐
Gave a verbal warning	☐
.... sanction given	☐
.... sanction given	☐
Student was moved away from friends	☐
Used positive reinforcement to get the student back on task	☐
Drew back from confrontation	☐
Student given 'time out' to calm down	☐

THE END?

If only! Perhaps it is just the beginning. Remember there is no quick fix. Take time to think how and with whom you are going to introduce the ideas in the handbook. Don't be surprised if you need to return to it a number of times while practising the strategies with your classes. Your students will also benefit from a gradual introduction and time to get to know the basics. Slowly you will find that you are able to negotiate elements of the practice with students, establish meaningful contracts for learning and involve them with managing and monitoring their own behaviour.

If you want more help, advice and training on advanced behaviour, classroom and assessment management just **ask@pivotaleducation.com** We offer courses, INSET and consultancy as well as our publications.

BIBLIOGRAPHY

Britton J, (1970) Language and Learning, London: Penguin Books.

Canter L, (1992) Assertive Discipline, Santa Monica CA: Lee Canter and Associates.

Goleman D, (1995.) Emotional Intelligence, New York: Bantam Books.

Gardner H, (1983) Frames of Mind, New York: Basic Books.

Vygotsky L, (1986 rev edition) Thought and Language, Massachusetts: MIT Press.

ACKNOWLEDGEMENTS AND CREDITS

Joe May, founding partner of Pivotal Education

Anne Denton and Year 8 at Worle School, Weston Super Mare

Ellie and Alison Wood

Graeme Rose - photographs

Simon Spencer, UCE, Birmingham

Geoff Anderson, Oxford Brookes University

Sue Smith, Manor Park School, Nuneaton

John Burton

Jack Black and Alfie Dix

Special thanks to Jules Mann for the artwork (www.beatbug.co.uk) and Pinstripe Print, Birmingham for the design.